DOMINOES

A Pretty Face

STARTER LEVEL 250 HEADWORDS

OXFORD
UNIVERSITY PRESS

Great Clarendon Street, Oxford OX2 6DP

Oxford University Press is a department of the University of Oxford.
It furthers the University's objective of excellence in research, scholarship, and education by publishing worldwide in

Oxford New York

Auckland Cape Town Dar es Salaam Hong Kong Karachi Kuala Lumpur Madrid Melbourne Mexico City Nairobi New Delhi Shanghai Taipei Toronto

With offices in

Argentina Austria Brazil Chile Czech Republic France Greece Guatemala Hungary Italy Japan Poland Portugal Singapore South Korea Switzerland Thailand Turkey Ukraine Vietnam

First published in Dominoes 2003

2023

15

ISBN: 978 0 19 424704 7 Book
ISBN: 978 0 19 463923 1 Book and Audio Pack

Printed in China

This book is printed on paper from certified and well-managed sources.

ACKNOWLEDGEMENTS

Illustrations by: Kanako Damerum and Yuzuru Takasaki

The publisher would like to thank the following for permission to reproduce the cover photograph:
Getty Images (portrait young woman/Tetra Images – Yuri Arcurs)

DOMINOES

Series Editors: Bill Bowler and Sue Parminter

A Pretty Face

John Escott

Illustrated by Kanako Damerum
and Yuzuru Takasaki

John Escott has written many books for readers of all ages, and particularly enjoys writing crime and mystery thrillers. He was born in the west of England, but now lives on the south coast. When he is not writing, he visits second-hand bookshops, watches videos of old Hollywood movies, and takes long walks along empty beaches. He has also written *The Wild West*, *Kidnap!* and *The Big Story*, and retold *William Tell and Other Stories* and *White Fang* for Dominoes.

OXFORD
UNIVERSITY PRESS

ACTIVITIES

BEFORE READING

Here are the people in the story *A Pretty Face*.

Zoe Baker

Aunt Peggy

Todd Marin

Mike Morrison

Annie O'Neil

Kate Lawson

1 Match these sentences with the pictures and write the names. Use a dictionary to help you.

a .... She's a student. She's Zoe's friend.

b .... She works in a bookstore. She likes acting.

c .... She's the editor of an important magazine.

d .... He's a student. He likes writing.

e .... He's a rich writer. He doesn't like talking to people.

f .... She's the editor of a small newspaper. She's Mike's aunt.

2 Some of the people in this story become friends. Who makes friends with who?

1 Zoe is angry

Zoe is seventeen years old. She works in a **bookstore**, in the little town of Newport. Zoe likes books and she likes her work. But after work she likes to **act** in **plays** with the Newport **Players**.

The Newport Players do six plays every year, and Zoe is in most of them. Some plays are exciting, and some plays are **famous**. This week, the play is *Romeo and Juliet* by William Shakespeare.

'A lot of people are coming to see it,' Zoe thinks. 'I must act well.'

bookstore a shop for books

act to speak and move; to tell a story in front of other people

play a story that people act

players an old name for people who act in plays

famous that everybody knows

college you study here after you leave school

theatre a building where people go to see plays

newspaper people read about things that happen every day in this

editor the person who says which stories go in a newspaper

review some writing in a newspaper telling people about a new play or book

Mike is eighteen years old. He is a student at Newport **College** and he likes writing. One day he wants to write plays for the **theatre** and for television.

'One day I want to be famous,' he thinks.

Newport has a **newspaper**. The *Newport Weekly News* is its name, and Mike's Aunt Peggy is the **editor**. One morning, she phones Mike.

'Do you want to write a **review** of *Romeo and Juliet* for the newspaper, Mike?' she asks him. 'The Newport Players are doing the play tonight at the Little Theatre.'

'Yes, please, Aunt Peggy!' Mike says. 'Thanks for asking me.'

That evening, he goes to Newport's Little Theatre to see the play.

Mike goes into the theatre and sits at the front. He gets out his **notebook** and pen, ready to write notes for his review. There are a lot of people in the **audience**.

Five minutes later, the play begins.

Zoe acts the **part** of Juliet's mother. She knows all her words and speaks them well.

Mike is watching her.

'She's very **pretty** and she's doing her best,' he thinks. 'But it's not easy to act the part of an older woman. She's only sixteen or seventeen years old, and we all know it.'

He begins to write in his notebook.

notebook a small book for writing in

audience the people who go to see a play

part one of the people in a play

pretty beautiful

Two hours later, the play ends and the audience leaves the theatre. Mike goes home and writes his review for the newspaper. He doesn't feel very happy.

'It was a good play, but what can I say about the girl acting the part of Juliet's mother?' he thinks. 'I want to be **kind** but I must be **honest**, too.'

At the bookstore on Friday, Zoe reads Mike's review of the play in the *Newport Weekly News.*

and Zoe Baker acts the part of Juliet's mother. She has a pretty face and she speaks her words well. But she is a young girl in an older woman's **costume**, and we all know it. She can never make me **believe** differently.

Zoe is angry. She looks at the name under the review: Mike Morrison.

'Who is this Mike Morrison?' she thinks. 'What does he know about acting?'

kind nice to people

honest saying things that are true

costume the things that a person wears in a play

believe to think that something is true

ACTIVITIES

READING CHECK

Choose the correct pictures.

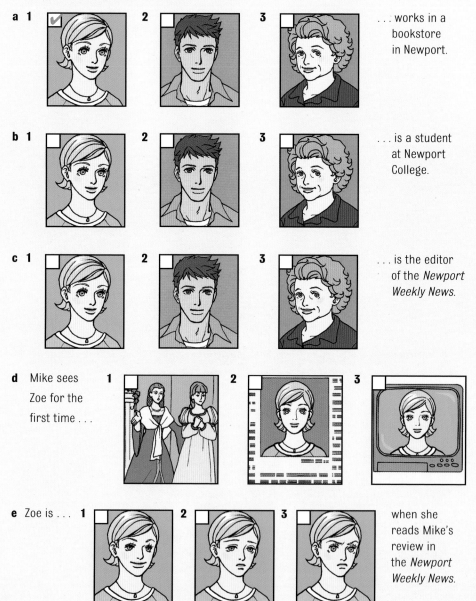

a **1**  **2**  **3**  . . . works in a bookstore in Newport.

b **1**  **2**  **3**  . . . is a student at Newport College.

c **1**  **2**  **3**  . . . is the editor of the *Newport Weekly News.*

d Mike sees Zoe for the first time . . . **1**  **2**  **3** 

e Zoe is . . . **1**  **2**  **3**  when she reads Mike's review in the *Newport Weekly News.*

ACTIVITIES

WORD WORK

1 These words don't match the pictures. Correct them.

a ~~newspaper~~ audience **b** audience .... **c** college ....

d notebook .... **e** costume .... **f** theatre ....

2 Use words from Chapter 1 to complete the sentences.

a Aunt Peggy is the e d i t o r of the *Newport Weekly News.*

b *Romeo and Juliet* is a _ _ _ _ by Shakespeare.

c Agatha Christie is a _ _ _ _ _ _ English writer.

d Zoe Baker likes to _ _ _ in her free time.

e Zoe has an important _ _ _ _ in this week's play – she is Juliet's mother.

f Mike thinks Zoe has a _ _ _ _ _ _ face.

g Mike must write a _ _ _ _ _ _ of *Romeo and Juliet* for Aunt Peggy's newspaper.

h Do you _ _ _ _ _ _ _ that Zoe can act well?

i Do you like my new shoes? Please be _ _ _ _ _ _ .

GUESS WHAT

What happens in the next chapter? Tick two boxes.

a ☐ Zoe sees Mike.

b ☐ Zoe talks to Mike.

c ☐ Zoe hits Mike.

d ☐ Zoe talks to a friend about Mike.

2 Zoe has an idea

On Tuesday evening the next week, Zoe and her friend Annie are drinking **coffee** in the Newport **Café**. Annie is a student at Newport College and sometimes in the evenings she and Zoe meet at the café.

Suddenly, Zoe sees a boy sitting at a table across the room. 'Who's that boy?' she asks Annie.

Annie laughs. 'Do you like him? He has a nice face,' she says. 'His name's Mike. I often see him at the college.'

'Mike?' Zoe says. 'Mike who?'

'Mike Morrison,' Annie says.

coffee people often drink this in the morning

café you go here to have a drink and something to eat

'That's Mike Morrison?' Zoe says. She is **furious**.

'Yes, why?' Annie asks.

'He writes reviews for the *Newport Weekly News,*' Zoe says.

'That's right,' Annie says. 'His aunt is the editor. He . . . oh!' She stops suddenly and looks at Zoe. 'The review of *Romeo and Juliet*—'

'Right!' Zoe says. 'Do you remember it? "Zoe Baker acts the part of Juliet's mother. She has a pretty face and she speaks her words well. But she is a young girl in an older woman's costume, and we all know it." Nice face or no nice face, I **hate** him!'

furious very angry

hate not to love

Annie laughs. 'OK, go and tell him,' she says. 'Go and say, "I hate you, Mike Morrison. You write **stupid** reviews for the newspaper." Go on.'

But Zoe isn't laughing. 'Yes, all right!' she says furiously, and she begins to get up from her chair. Then she stops, suddenly.

'What's wrong?' Annie asks. 'Are you afraid?'

'No,' Zoe says. 'I have a better **idea**. Does he come into this café often?'

'Every Tuesday and Thursday evening, I think,' Annie says. 'He has a writing **class** at the college, and he comes here after it finishes.'

stupid without thinking well

idea something that you think

class a time when students learn with a teacher

Zoe thinks for a minute or two. 'That's very interesting,' she says at last.

'Is it?' Annie says. She looks across at Mike Morrison, then at Zoe. 'Why is it interesting? What are you thinking of doing?'

'Tell me, am I a good **actress**?' Zoe asks.

'Yes, you are,' Annie says. 'But—'

'OK,' Zoe says. 'I'm a good actress and I want to **prove** it to Mr Mike-Nice-Face-Morrison.'

'How do you want to do that?' Annie asks.

Zoe smiles and begins to tell Annie about her idea . . .

actress a woman who acts in plays

prove to make people see that something is true

READING CHECK

Put these sentences in the correct order. Number them 1–8.

- **a** ☐ Zoe gets very angry.
- **b** ☐ Zoe sees a boy across the room.
- **c** ☐ Annie remembers the review of *Romeo and Juliet.*
- **d** ☐ Zoe starts to get up to speak to Mike.
- **e** 1 Zoe and Annie meet at the Newport Café.
- **f** ☐ In the end Zoe wants to do something and she tells Annie about it.
- **g** ☐ Then Zoe sits down again.
- **h** ☐ Annie says the boy's name is Mike Morrison.

WORD WORK

1 Find nine more words from Chapter 2 in the computer.

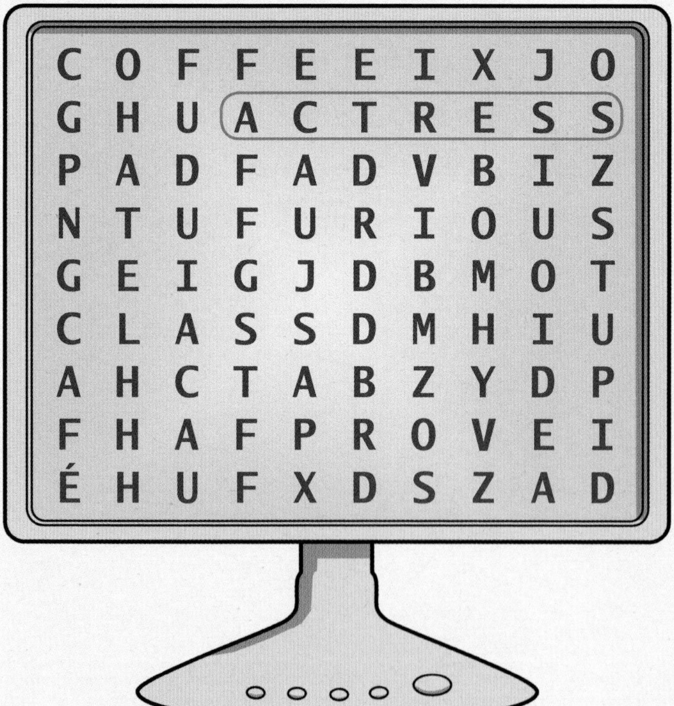

C	O	F	F	E	E	I	X	J	O
G	H	U	(A	C	T	R	E	S	S)
P	A	D	F	A	D	V	B	I	Z
N	T	U	F	U	R	I	O	U	S
G	E	I	G	J	D	B	M	O	T
C	L	A	S	S	D	M	H	I	U
A	H	C	T	A	B	Z	Y	D	P
F	H	A	F	P	R	O	V	E	I
É	H	U	F	X	D	S	Z	A	D

2 Use the words from Activity 1 to complete these sentences.

a Zoe's a good actress....... and she wants to p.................. it.

b My father loves drinking c.................. in the morning, but I h.................. it.

c At my college we have an English c.................. every week.

d Zoe doesn't like Mike Morrison's review – she thinks it's a s.................. review and she is f.................. with him!

e At the end of the chapter, Zoe has an i..................; she wants to do something.

f A c.................. is a good place to meet friends.

GUESS WHAT

What happens in the next chapter? Tick one box.

a ☐ Someone phones Aunt Peggy.

b ☐ Mike meets a famous writer.

c ☐ Mike meets an editor.

d ☐ Zoe meets a famous actress.

3 A difficult interview

On Thursday, Mike comes to the Newport Café after his writing class.

He asks for a cup of coffee, then starts to read one of his books. Some minutes later, a woman comes into the café. She is **carrying** a **magazine** under her arm.

At first, Mike does not see the woman. Then she comes across to his table.

'Hello,' she says. 'Are you Mike Morrison?'

Mike is **surprised**. 'Yes,' he says. 'That's me.'

The woman smiles. 'Can I sit at this table?' she asks.

'Yes, of course,' Mike says.

carry to take

magazine a thin book with lots of pictures in it; you can buy it every week or every month

surprised feeling that something very new is suddenly happening

'My name is Kate Lawson,' the woman says. 'I'm the editor of *Yes!* magazine. Do you know it?'

She sits down and puts the magazine on the table in front of Mike.

'Yes, I know it,' Mike says. 'It's a magazine about famous people.'

'That's right,' Kate says. 'Do you want to write something for it? Can you do an **interview** for me?'

interview a meeting to ask questions

'An interview?' Mike says, surprised. 'Why are you asking me?'

'You sometimes write theatre reviews for the Newport weekly newspaper,' she says. 'Is that right?'

'Yes, I do,' he says. 'I want to write plays one day, and—'

'Well, do this interview for my magazine then,' she says. 'It's with a famous **playwright**. He lives in Newport.'

'Todd Marin is the only famous playwright in Newport,' Mike says. 'He lives quietly and doesn't go out very often. And he's famous for not talking to **reporters** from . . . **gossip** magazines. He **throws** them **out** of his house!'

playwright a person who writes plays

reporter a person who writes for a newspaper or magazine

gossip talking openly about people's lives

throw out to make somebody leave a building

Kate laughs. 'Are you afraid?' she says. 'Good reporters aren't afraid to do **difficult** interviews. You want to write plays, don't you? Well, perhaps he can tell you something about play-writing.'

Mike thinks, 'She's right. Perhaps I can learn something from Todd Marin.'

'OK!' he says. 'When can I do it?'

'Tomorrow morning,' Kate says. 'You must tell Marin, "This interview is for *Yes!* magazine." But tell him after you get into the house. OK?'

'OK,' Mike says.

difficult not easy

ACTIVITIES

READING CHECK

Match the first and second parts of these sentences.

a Mike is . . .
b A woman comes . . .
c She comes across . . .
d First she says . . .
e Then she says 'I'm . . .
f She puts a magazine . . .
g She asks Mike . . .
h Mike must do an interview . . .
i Mike says . . .

1 into the café.
2 the editor of *Yes!* magazine.'
3 drinking a cup of coffee at the Newport Café.
4 'Can you write something for *Yes!*?'
5 to Mike's table and sits down.
6 'yes'.
7 with Todd Marin, the famous playwright.
8 on the table in front of Mike.
9 'My name is Kate Lawson.'

WORD WORK

1 Find words from Chapter 3 in the coffee cups.

a

carry

b

s _ _ _ _ _ _ _ _

c

p _ _ _ _ _ _ _ _ _

d

g _ _ _ _ _

e

m _ _ _ _ _ _ _

f

d _ _ _ _ _ _ _ _

g

r _ _ _ _ _ _ _

h

i _ _ _ _ _ _ _ _

ACTIVITIES

2 Use the words from Activity 1 to complete the sentences.

a Shakespeare is a famous English playwright .

b *Newsweek* is a famous American ....

c I'd like to be a .... and write for a newspaper.

d It's .... to be a good writer.

e Mike must do an .... with Todd Marin tomorrow.

f Mike is .... when Kate Lawson says his name.

g Some magazines have a lot of .... about famous people in them.

GUESS WHAT

What happens in the next chapter? Read the sentences and write *Yes* or *No*.

a Zoe phones Annie. ....

b Zoe phones Kate. ....

c Mike meets Todd Marin. ....

d Todd throws Mike out. ....

4 Todd Marin's house

Later that evening, Zoe is speaking to Annie on the phone.

'. . . so I say to him, "I'm the editor of *Yes!* magazine and can you interview Todd Marin?"' Zoe tells Annie.

'Todd Marin!' Annie says. 'But he throws gossip magazine reporters out of his house!'

'I know!' Zoe says, laughing. 'And I want to stand outside his house and watch Todd Marin throw Mike Morrison out!'

The next morning, Mike goes to Todd Marin's house. It is a big house, and there are lots of **bushes** and tall trees in front of it.

'I don't like *Yes!* magazine very much, but this is an important interview,' Mike thinks. 'And perhaps I can talk to Todd Marin about my play.' (Mike is writing a play for television.)

He walks up to the front door of the house. He is carrying his notebook and he has a **list** of questions to ask the playwright. But he is a little afraid of the famous man.

bush a short, little tree

list a number of things that you write down

follow to go after someone

wig false hair

glasses you wear these to help you see better

hide to go where no one can see you

funny making you laugh

Zoe **follows** Mike to Todd Marin's house. She is careful and she follows Mike very quietly. Zoe is acting the part of Kate Lawson again. She has a black **wig** over her hair and she is wearing **glasses**.

She **hides** behind one of the bushes in front of Todd Marin's house and watches Mike go to the front door. It is a big, dark house.

'This is **funny**,' she thinks, smiling.

When Todd Marin opens the door of his house, Mike begins to talk quickly.

'Hello, Mr Marin,' he says. 'I'm Mike Morrison. I'm a student at Newport College, and I want to write plays.'

'Do you?' Todd Marin says.

'And I write reviews in the *Newport Weekly News*,' Mike tells him.

'What do you want from me?' Todd Marin asks.

'Can I ask you some questions?' Mike says.

'Why?' Marin asks. 'Is it for the *Newport Weekly News?*'

'That's a difficult question. What do I do now?' Mike thinks. 'Do I tell him a **lie**, or do I tell him the **truth**?' Then, after a second or two, he says, 'It . . . it's for *Yes!* magazine. Listen, I know it's a stupid magazine, but . . .'

'Come into the house,' Todd Marin says suddenly.

lie something that is not true

truth something that is true

READING CHECK

Correct six more mistakes in the story.

Zoe speaks to ~~Mike~~ Annie on the phone that evening. She tells her friend about Kate Lawson and she cries. The next morning, Mike goes to Todd Marin's office. Mike likes *Yes!* magazine, but the interview with Todd Marin is important; he knows that. Zoe watches Mike go to the front door. She is acting the part of Juliet's mother. Mike and Todd talk at the front door. Mike says, 'I'm writing for the *Newport Weekly News*.' Todd says to Mike 'Go away!'

WORD WORK

Complete the sentences with words from Chapter 4.

a It's a bad idea to tell a ......lie........ .

b Zoe hides behind a ....

c My grandmother has white hair; she's wearing a .... !

d I like this play. It's ....

e When you can't remember things, it's good to write a ....

f My dogs .... me to school every day.

g I can .... and you can look for me.

GUESS WHAT

What happens in the next chapter? Tick the boxes.

a Todd Marin . . .
- **1** ☐ throws Mike out of his house.
- **2** ☐ talks to Mike in his study.
- **3** ☐ gives Mike a play to read.

b Todd Marin says yes . . .
- **1** ☐ to an interview for *Yes!* magazine.
- **2** ☐ to an interview for the *Newport Weekly News*.
- **3** ☐ to reading Mike's play.

c Zoe waits . . .
- **1** ☐ for more than an hour.
- **2** ☐ in her car.
- **3** ☐ in Todd Marin's house.

d Todd Marin and Mike talk about . . .
- **1** ☐ Todd's plays.
- **2** ☐ Mike's play.
- **3** ☐ gossip magazines.

5 Zoe waits

Zoe is watching Mike and Todd Marin from behind a bush. She can see them but she cannot hear them speaking. She sees Todd Marin open the door, and she sees Mike follow him into the house.

Zoe smiles. 'Right. He's in the house,' she thinks. 'Now let's wait for Todd Marin to throw him out!'

Todd Marin takes Mike to his **study**. There are hundreds of books in the room, and a big **desk**. Todd goes and sits behind the desk.

'Thank you for telling me the truth,' he says to Mike. 'I can see you're an honest young man. You can ask your questions. But not for *Yes!* magazine. You're right. It is a stupid magazine. I hate gossip magazines. Why do people write for them?'

'Because they **pay** a lot of money, I believe,' Mike says.

Todd Marin laughs. 'Yes, you're right again,' he says. 'But you can write about me for the *Newport Weekly News*. Is that OK?'

'Yes, that's OK,' Mike says, and he smiles at Todd Marin happily.

'I like to help young writers with ideas when I can,' Todd says kindly. 'Sit down.'

Mike sits down, puts his notebook on Todd's desk, and opens it.

'I read your reviews in the newspaper sometimes,' Todd says. 'They're very good.'

'Well, I think they're OK,' Mike says. 'But I want to write for the theatre, for TV, and for **movies**. I'm writing a play now.'

'Are you? Tell me about it,' Todd says.

'Can I?' Mike asks. 'Well, it's about a boy and a girl.'

'A boy and a girl?'

'That's right. They . . .'

Todd Marin sits back in his chair to listen and Mike tells him the **plot** of his play. Mike is very **nervous**, but Todd Marin does not speak. He smiles at Mike and he listens to him very carefully.

study a room in a house where you go to write or work

desk a table in a study or in an office

pay to give money for something

movie moving pictures that tell a story

plot the story of a book, play, or movie

nervous a little afraid

When at last Mike stops speaking, Todd says, 'Thank you. That's very interesting. It's a good story, and it's funny too. But there are one or two things you can do to make it better. To begin with . . .'

Zoe stays behind the bush and waits. An hour goes by and nothing happens. She is getting **impatient**.

'What are they doing in there?' she thinks. 'Todd Marin never gives interviews to gossip magazines, so what are they talking about?'

She remembers Mike Morrison's review of *Romeo and Juliet* in the newspaper. She remembers his words about her acting – and she wants to see his face when Todd Marin throws him out of the house.

'How long must I wait?' she thinks impatiently.

impatient not feeling happy about waiting for something

READING CHECK

1 Correct the mistakes.

a Zoe watches Mike and Todd Marin from behind a ~~car~~ bush.

b Todd Marin takes Mike to the café.

c Todd Marin likes gossip magazines.

d Todd Marin likes to help old writers.

e Mike photographs Todd Marin for the *Newport Weekly News*.

f Todd Marin asks Mike about his friends.

g Zoe waits in front of Todd Marin's study for more than an hour.

h Zoe remembers Mike's review of *Antony and Cleopatra*.

2 Are these sentences true or false? Tick the boxes.	**True**	**False**
a Zoe can hear Mike and Todd Marin talking.	☐	☑
b Todd Marin likes Mike because he is honest.	☐	☐
c Mike is going to write about Todd Marin for *Yes!* magazine.	☐	☐
d Mike is writing a play about a boy and a girl.	☐	☐
e Todd Marin throws Mike out of the house.	☐	☐

ACTIVITIES

WORD WORK

Use the words from the front door to complete the sentences.

a I'm not happy about speaking in front of lots of people. I'm usually very ..nervous....

b This is my .... I do all my writing in this room.

c He has a big .... with a computer on it.

d This book has a very interesting .... It's about a man going back in time.

e People sometimes get .... when they are waiting for the bus.

f 'You don't have any money! That's OK. I can .... for our coffees.'

g Mike is writing a play, but he wants to write for TV and .... too.

GUESS WHAT

What happens in the next chapter? Tick three boxes.

a ☐ Zoe is tired of waiting and she goes home.

b ☐ Mike leaves Todd Marin's house with a smile on his face.

c ☐ Kate Lawson is angry with Mike.

d ☐ Mike writes a play for the Newport Players to perform.

e ☐ Mike and Zoe make friends.

f ☐ Annie tells Mike the truth about Kate Lawson.

6 Telling the truth

After an hour and a half, Mike Morrison leaves Todd Marin's study and comes out of the house. He and the playwright are smiling, and Mike is saying 'Thank you.'

They talk for two or three minutes and Zoe watches them from behind the bush. She is **amazed**.

'What's happening?' she thinks. 'Why are they so friendly?'

After a minute or two more, they **shake hands**. Then Todd Marin goes back into the house and Mike Morrison walks away.

amazed very surprised

shake hands to give your hand to someone when you say hello or goodbye to them

Mike sees Kate Lawson waiting for him.

'Oh, hello,' he says nervously. He is surprised to see her so soon. 'Are you waiting for me?'

'Yes,' she says impatiently. 'I'm waiting for your interview.'

'Look, I can't lie to you,' he replies. 'There's no interview for *Yes!* magazine. Mr Marin always **refuses** to talk to reporters from gossip magazines.'

'But what—?' Kate begins.

'What can two people talk about for an hour and a half?' Mike says, laughing. 'About writing, about **characters** and about plot. Nothing for *Yes!* magazine, I'm afraid. Oh,

refuse to say no when someone asks you to do something

character a person in a book, a movie or a play

I have my list of questions and Mr Marin's answers, but my interview is for the *Newport Weekly News*. And I know a lot more about writing plays now. He's very interested in my play.'

'*Your play?*' Kate says furiously.

'Yes, I'm writing a play for TV,' Mike says. 'And Mr Marin wants to read it. He can help me with the characters and the plot.'

'Well, that's nice,' she says. 'Say hello to Mike Morrison, the famous playwright! He writes stupid reviews for the *Newport Weekly News* but his plays are OK.'

'You're angry,' Mike says. 'Listen, I'm sorry about the interview for *Yes!*'

Kate laughs. 'No, it's OK,' she says. 'I'm not angry.' And then she does something very strange.

She takes off her hair.

'She's wearing a wig!' Mike thinks, amazed.

Next, she takes off her glasses and she smiles at Mike.

And now he knows her.

He begins to laugh. 'You're not Kate Lawson!' he says. 'You're—'

'That's right,' Zoe says. 'I'm a seventeen-year-old girl in an older woman's costume, Mr Mike Morrison, review writer for the *Newport Weekly News*!'

Mike's face is very red now. He feels **embarrassed**. 'What a **trick**! So there is no Kate Lawson, editor of *Yes!* magazine,' he says.

'No, there isn't,' Zoe says, laughing. 'What do you think now? Does this prove something? Am I a good actress?'

'Yes, you are a good actress,' Mike says, laughing with her. 'And I'm going to put that in the *Newport Weekly News*.'

'Are you?' Zoe says.

'Yes, and thanks for making me go and see Todd Marin,' Mike tells her. He doesn't feel embarrassed any more.

'Now I can get help with my play,' he says. 'Come on, let's get a cup of coffee. And I'm paying!'

'Well, I can't refuse a **free** coffee!' Zoe says, and she laughs.

embarrassed feeling bad after you do something stupid

trick something that you do to make somebody feel stupid

free that you don't pay for

The End

ACTIVITIES

READING CHECK

Write sentences about Chapter 6.

a After an hour and a half  leaves  's house.

After an hour and a half Mike leaves Todd Marin's house.

b Mike and Todd Marin are  .

....

c Mike sees Kate waiting in front of Todd Marin's  .

....

d Mike tells her about Marin helping him with his 

.

....

e  takes off her  and  .

....

f Mike is now talking to  – not  .

....

g In the end Mike and Zoe are friends and they go for a  .

....

WORD WORK

Use the words in the glasses to complete the sentences.

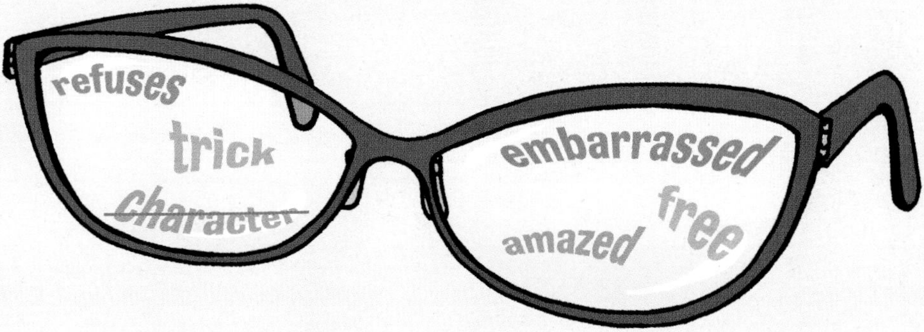

a Romeo is an important character in Shakespeare's play *Romeo and Juliet.*

b You don't need to pay for this ticket. It's ....

c Zoe puts on a wig and glasses to play a .... on Mike Morrison.

d Mike is .... when Kate takes off her hair and he sees it's a wig.

e Todd Marin .... to give interviews for gossip magazines.

f Mike is .... and his face is red when he thinks about his review of *Romeo and Juliet.*

GUESS WHAT

What happens after the story ends? Choose from these ideas or add your own.

a ☐ Todd Marin helps Mike with his play.

b ☐ Mike writes a play for Zoe.

c ☐ Mike visits Zoe in her bookstore every day.

d ☐ Aunt Peggy meets Todd Marin and likes him a lot.

e ☐ Annie and Zoe stop being friends.

f ☐ ....

g ☐ ....

Project A *A Newspaper Report*

1 Correct the underlined words in this newspaper report.

NEWPORT WEEKLY NEWS

ACTRESS'S TRICK ON REVIEW WRITER

Zoe Baker works in a supermarket in Newport. She acts in plays with the Newport Players too. This week she acts the part of Romeo's mother in *Romeo and Juliet* at the Big Theatre, Newport. She says, 'I like acting in plays, and I like acting younger characters. I'm only seven years old.'

Mike Morrison is a teacher at Newport College. He sometimes writes stories for the *Newport Weekly News*. (His Aunt Kate is the editor of the newspaper.) He likes writing books in his free time.

2 Put these words in order to write more of the report.

a glasses | Zoe Baker | and | a wig | puts on | .

Zoe Baker puts on a wig and glasses.

b *Yes!* magazine | She's | under her arm | carrying | .

....

c of *Yes!*' | 'I'm | says, | She | the editor

....

d Kate Lawson,' | says | she | 'My name's | .

....

e She | with Todd Marin?' | 'Can you do an interview | asks | Mike Morrison,

....

3 Put these sentences in order to finish the report. Number them 1–7.

a ☐ She watches Mike and Todd Marin from behind a bush.

b ☐ The next morning Mike Morrison goes to Todd Marin's house.

c ☐ Mike comes out of Todd Marin's house and he sees Kate Lawson.

d ☐ Mike remembers his review of *Romeo and Juliet* and he feels embarrassed.

e ☐ Zoe acts the part of Kate Lawson and follows Mike.

f ☐ Zoe takes off her wig and glasses.

g ☐ Now Mike Morrison says, 'You're a good actress, Zoe Baker!'

Project B Writing a Play

1 Use Zoe's words to complete this scene from Chapter 2 of the story.

I have a better idea.
He writes reviews for the *Newport Weekly News*.
Yes, all right.
Nice face or no nice face, I hate him!
Mike who?

SCENE 2

In Newport Café

Zoe and Annie are talking. Mike is sitting across the room.

Zoe looks over and sees Mike. She is interested in him.

ZOE *(to Annie, quietly)* Who's that boy?

ANNIE *(laughing)* Do you like him? He has a nice face. His name's Mike. He goes to Newport College with me.

ZOE Mike? **(a)** ....

ANNIE Mike Morrison.

ZOE *(surprised)* That's Mike Morrison!

ANNIE Yes, why?

ZOE **(b)** ....

ANNIE That's right. He . . . oh! The review of Romeo and Juliet—

ZOE *(angrily)* Right! You remember it?

(c) ....

ANNIE *(laughing)* OK, go and say 'I hate you, Mike Morrison. You write stupid reviews for the newspaper.' Go on.

ZOE *(furiously)* **(d)** ....

ANNIE What's wrong? Are you afraid?

ZOE No. **(e)** ....

2 Use Mike's words to complete this scene from Chapter 4.

Listen, I know it's a stupid magazine, but—
Can I ask you some questions?
It ... It's for *Yes!* magazine.
And I write reviews in the *Newport Weekly News*.
Hello Mr Marin. I'm Mike Morrison and I want to write plays.

SCENE 4

At Todd Marin's House

Mike is standing in front of the house. Todd Marin opens the door.

MIKE *(excitedly)* **(a)** ....

TODD *(interested)* Do you?

MIKE **(b)** ....

TODD What do you want from me?

MIKE *(nervously)* **(c)** ....

TODD Why? Is it for the Newport Weekly News?

MIKE *(after a second or two)* **(d)** ....

Todd Marin looks furiously at Mike and begins to close the door.

MIKE *(quickly)* **(e)** ....

Todd Marin opens the door again.

TODD *(suddenly)* Come into the house.

3 Act out the scenes on page 42 and 43 before you look at page 44.

4 Look at four more scenes from the story. Write one scene and act it out.

SCENE 1

In the newspaper office

SCENE 3

On the phone

SCENE 5

In Todd Marin's study

SCENE 6

In Newport Café

GRAMMAR CHECK

Adverbs of frequency

We use adverbs of frequency to say how often something happens.

always usually often sometimes never

In Present Simple sentences, adverbs of frequency go in front of most verbs, but after the verb *to be*.

Mike Morrison never goes to college on Sundays.

Todd Marin is usually in his study in the mornings.

1 Write the sentences again. Use the correct adverb.

a Todd reads Mike's reviews in the paper. (usually/sometimes)

Todd sometimes reads Mike's review in the paper.

b Zoe acts in plays with the Newport Players. (always/usually)

....

c Todd throws reporters from gossip magazines out of his house. (often/always)

....

d Todd gives interviews to reporters from gossip magazines. (usually/never)

....

e Mike comes to the café after class on Tuesdays and Thursdays. (usually/sometimes)

....

f Mike writes reviews for the *Newport Weekly News*. (always/sometimes)

....

g Zoe meets Annie in the café at Newport College. (often/sometimes)

....

h Annie sees Mike at Newport College. (often/never)

....

i Zoe goes to classes at Newport College. (always/never)

....

j Todd is kind to young writers. (always/sometimes)

....

GRAMMAR

GRAMMAR CHECK

Time clauses with at, in, on, this, that, every, next, and later

We use at with clock times, in with parts of the day, and on with days.

at six o'clock *in the afternoon*

on Monday *on Monday afternoon*

We do not use a preposition before this, that, every, and next.

The Newport Players are doing a play this evening.

That afternoon, Zoe speaks to Annie on the phone.

Zoe works in a bookstore every day.

The next morning, Mike goes to Todd Marin's house.

We can use later to mean *after that time*.

Annie arrives at six o'clock, and leaves ten minutes later.

2 Complete the text. Use *at, in, on,* or no preposition (–), *later* or *the*.

a) ..On.. Monday Zoe is starting work b) .... nine o'clock c) .... the morning. d) .... half past eleven she is meeting Jackie for coffee. She is reading a play with the Newport Players e) .... that evening. She meets them f) .... every Monday. Two hours g) .... she is meeting Mike for a drink. h) .... next morning Zoe is starting work i) .... eleven o'clock. j) .... the afternoon she is phoning Annie k) .... four o'clock, and she is finishing work one hour l) .... m) .... the evening she is watching a movie with Mike n) .... eight o'clock.

MONDAY

9:00 am	start work
11:30 am	meet Jackie for coffee
7:30 pm	read play with Newport Players
9:30 pm	meet Mike for drink

TUESDAY

11:00 am	start work
4:00 pm	phone Annie
5:00 pm	finish work
8:00 pm	watch movie with Mike

GRAMMAR CHECK

Subject pronouns

We use subject pronouns – I, you, he, she, it, we, and they – to replace subject nouns. Subject pronouns go in front of the main verb.

Zoe works in a bookstore.	*She works in a bookstore.*
Mike is a student.	*He is a student.*
Zoe and Annie are having coffee.	*They are having coffee.*

3 Choose the correct subject pronouns to complete the letter.

Andy Page
1 High Street
Newport

The Editor
Newport Weekly News

Dear Editor
a) (I/You) ..I.. always go to the Little Theatre with my family to see the Newport Players. b) (They/You) .... are very good, and c) (you/we) .... like their plays very much. But Mike Morrison does not like all the Players.
d) (I/He) .... says, 'Zoe Baker is a young woman in an older woman's costume, and e) (they/we) .... all know it.' Well, what does f) (he/she) .... know about acting?
g) (She/You) is a good actress, and when h) (we/they) see her in the play, i) (she/we) .... is Juliet's mother.
I think that j) (you/she) .... need a different person to write reviews! k) (They/I) .... don't want to read more reviews by Mike Morrison. l) (They/He) .... must watch more plays, and think more. Then m) (we/he) can write better reviews!
Yours faithfully
Andy Page

GRAMMAR CHECK

Sequencing words: at first, then, later, in the end, and at the same time

We use sequencing words to show the order of events in a story. Sequencing words usually come at the beginning of a sentence. To start a story, we use at first. To link actions that happen at different times, we can use then or later. To show that something took a long time, or to end a story, we can use in the end.

At first, Aunt Peggy asks Mike to write a review. Then, he goes to the theatre. Later, he watches Zoe as Juliet's mother. In the end, he writes his review for the newspaper.

When two things happen together, we can use at the same time.

At the same time, Zoe and Annie see Mike in the café.

4 Put the sentences in the correct order. Then complete the sentences with the sequencing words in the box.

~~at first~~	in the end	later	then

a .... Annie talks to Zoe about Mike Morrison.

b .... she plays a trick on Mike.

c ..1... ..At first.. Zoe meets Annie in the café at Newport College.

d .... Zoe has an idea.

5 Match the sentence halves correctly.

a At first Mike

b Then Todd

c At the same time Kate

d Later Mike

e In the end Zoe

1 watches from behind the bushes.

2 takes off Kate's glasses and wig.

3 goes to Todd Marin's house.

4 leaves Todd's house with his interview.

5 comes to the door and speaks to him.

GRAMMAR CHECK

Adverbs

We use some adverbs to talk about how something is done.

Mike is a quick writer. He writes quickly.

We make these adverbs from adjectives by adding –ly.

nervous – nervously *impatient – impatiently*

For adjectives that end in consonant + –y, we change the y to i and add –ly.

Zoe is happy when she smiles at Mike. She smiles happily.

Some adverbs are irregular.

good – well

6 Complete the sentences. Use adverbs made from the adjectives in the box.

angry	good	careful	~~honest~~	impatient
furious	kind	nervous	quick	quiet

a Mike says true things about the play. He writes honestly .

b Todd Marin does not see many people. He lives ....

c Mike is a little afraid of Todd Marin. He speaks to him ....

d Zoe stands behind the bushes for a long time, but nothing happens. She waits ....

e Mike wants to write the review very much. He says yes ....

f Zoe hates Mike's review. She reads it ....

g Zoe does not want Mike to see her. She follows him ....

h Todd wants to help Mike. He speaks to him ....

i Zoe is very angry when she sees Mike in the café. She talks to Annie .... about Mike's review.

j Todd likes Mike's reviews. Mike writes .... , he thinks.

GRAMMAR CHECK

Time clauses with before, after, and when

Before links a later action with an earlier action.

Before Zoe acts in a play, she learns her words.

After links an earlier action with a later action.

After Zoe meets Annie, she sees Mike in the café.

When links two actions close in time, where the first action happens just before the second action. Sometimes the second action is a result of the first action.

When Zoe gets to Todd's house, she hides behind the bushes.

We can put *before*, *after*, and *when* clauses at the end of the sentence. In this case, we do not use a comma.

Zoe learns her words before she acts in a play.

Zoe sees Mike in the café after she meets Annie.

Zoe hides behind the bushes when she gets to Todd's house.

7 Complete the sentences. Use the words in the box.

when	After	before	when	After	When
Before	When	~~after~~	before	after	

a Zoe goes to the theatre after she finishes work.
b .... Mike sits down, *Romeo and Juliet* begins.
c Mike begins to write in his notebook .... he sees Zoe in the play.
d .... Zoe and Annie see Mike, they drink some coffee in the café.
e Zoe learns about Mike from Annie .... she has her idea.
f .... Kate Lawson talks to Mike, he goes to talk to Todd Marin.
g .... Mike tells Todd the truth, Todd asks him into the house.
h Kate meets Mike outside the house .... Todd helps Mike with his play.
i Mike says 'I'm sorry!' .... Kate takes off her wig and glasses.
j .... Zoe tells Mike about her trick, he feels very embarrassed.
k .... Mike and Zoe go for coffee, they are friends.

GRAMMAR

GRAMMAR CHECK

Plural nouns

We usually add –s to singular nouns to make plural nouns.

note – notes   *coffee – coffees*   *day – days*

When a noun ends in –sh, –ch, –s, –ss, –x, or –z, we add –es to make the plural.

bush – bushes   *class – classes*

When a noun ends in consonant + –y, we change the y to i and add –es

body – bodies

Some nouns have irregular plurals.

man – men   *woman – women*   *person – people*

8 Write these words in the correct plural form. Then complete the sentences with the correct words.

actress	play ....
coffee	study ....
boy	glass glasses
story	reporter ....
character	person ....

a Zoe puts on a wig and glasses.
b Annie gets two .... : one for Zoe and one for her.
c Todd Marin does not like .... from gossip magazines.
d Playwrights often do their work in their ....
e In his writing class Mike writes .... for television.
f Zoe is one of the best .... in the Newport Players.
g There are a lot of .... in the audience.
h In the bookstore there are books of .... for children.
i Lots of .... and girls are students at Newport College.
j *Romeo and Juliet* is a play with lots of ....

DOMINOES Your Choice

Read *Dominoes* for pleasure, or to develop language skills. It's your choice.

Each *Domino* reader includes:

- a good story to enjoy
- integrated activities to develop reading skills and increase vocabulary
- task-based projects – perfect for CEFR portfolios
- contextualized grammar activities

Each *Domino* pack contains a reader, and an excitingly dramatized audio recording of the story

If you liked this *Domino*, read these:

Kidnap!

John Escott

One cold winter morning, a famous movie star and her teenage daughter are driving along a country road . . .

A blue van is waiting for them. Tom is in the van, but he's not a kidnapper – he's an artist. He usually draws pictures for adventure stories. Now he's in a real life adventure.

Rip Van Winkle & The Legend of Sleepy Hollow

Washington Irving

In the first of these stories, Rip Van Winkle sleeps for over twenty years, and then wakes up to a world that he no longer understands. In the other story, Ichabod Crane, the school teacher, meets a headless rider in the middle of a dark night. These two classic tales of the supernatural by Washington Irving have been popular for nearly two hundred years.

	CEFR	Cambridge Exams	IELTS	TOEFL iBT	TOEIC
Level 3	B1	PET	4.0	57-86	550
Level 2	A2–B1	KET-PET	3.0-4.0	–	390
Level 1	A1–A2	YLE Flyers/KET	3.0	–	225
Starter & Quick Starter	A1	YLE Movers	1.0–2.0	–	–